EMMANUEL JOSEPH

From Layoff to Lift Up: Career Recovery Map

Copyright © 2025 by Emmanuel Joseph

All rights reserved. No part of this publication may be reproduced, stored or transmitted in any form or by any means, electronic, mechanical, photocopying, recording, scanning, or otherwise without written permission from the publisher. It is illegal to copy this book, post it to a website, or distribute it by any other means without permission.

First edition

*This book was professionally typeset on Reedsy.
Find out more at reedsy.com*

Contents

1	Chapter 1	1
2	Chapter 1: The Shock of Layoff	4
3	Chapter 2: Redefining Your Career Goals	6
4	Chapter 3: Crafting Your Personal Brand	8
5	Chapter 4: Navigating the Job Market	10
6	Chapter 5: Leveraging Gig Economy and Freelancing	12
7	Chapter 6: Exploring Alternative Career Paths	14
8	Chapter 7: Building a Support System	16
9	Chapter 8: Preparing for Interviews	18
10	Chapter 9: Negotiating Job Offers	20
11	Chapter 10: Onboarding and Settling In	22
12	Chapter 11: Continuous Learning and Growth	24
13	Chapter 12: Embracing the Future	26

1

Chapter 1

Introduction

The journey of a career is often compared to a winding road with unexpected turns, detours, and roadblocks. One such roadblock that many professionals encounter is a layoff. The word itself can evoke a sense of dread, uncertainty, and even failure. However, it is crucial to remember that a layoff is not the end of the road but rather a challenging bend that requires resilience, adaptation, and a well-crafted recovery plan. This book, "From Layoff to Lift Up: Career Recovery Map," is designed to guide you through the process of bouncing back from a layoff and emerging stronger, more focused, and ready for new opportunities.

Experiencing a layoff can be an emotional rollercoaster. The initial shock, followed by a wave of emotions ranging from anger to sadness, can be overwhelming. It is essential to allow yourself the space to process these emotions and understand that it is a natural response to a significant life change. This book will offer practical advice on managing the emotional impact of a layoff and finding ways to stay positive and motivated.

One of the first steps in career recovery is redefining your goals. A layoff presents a unique opportunity to take a step back and reflect on what you truly want from your professional life. Are you passionate about your current industry, or is it time to explore new fields? This book will help you assess your strengths, identify new career paths, and set meaningful objectives that align with your values and aspirations.

Personal branding has become increasingly important in today's competitive job market. How you present yourself to potential employers can significantly impact your job search success. From crafting a compelling resume to building a strong online presence, this book will provide you with the tools and strategies to create a personal brand that stands out and resonates with your target audience.

Navigating the job market after a layoff can be daunting, but it is a journey that you do not have to undertake alone. Networking, both online and offline, plays a crucial role in uncovering job opportunities and gaining valuable insights. This book will guide you on how to effectively leverage your network, build new connections, and tap into the hidden job market to accelerate your job search.

The gig economy and freelancing offer alternative pathways to financial stability and professional growth. Embracing these options can provide flexibility and diverse work experiences that enhance your skillset. This book will explore the benefits of freelancing, how to find gig opportunities, and strategies for building a successful freelance career.

Transitioning to a new career or industry can be a daunting prospect, especially after a layoff. However, it can also be an exciting opportunity for growth and reinvention. This book will help you identify transferable skills, explore new industries, and develop a strategic plan for a successful career transition. By staying open to new possibilities, you can turn a layoff into a stepping stone for a fulfilling and rewarding career.

Building a support system is vital during this challenging period. Friends, family, mentors, and career coaches can provide invaluable advice, encouragement, and perspective. This book will emphasize the importance of seeking support, engaging in self-care, and maintaining a positive mindset. With the right guidance and a proactive approach, you can navigate the complexities of career recovery and emerge stronger and more resilient.

"From Layoff to Lift Up: Career Recovery Map" is not just a guidebook; it is a companion on your journey to career recovery. Each chapter is filled with

CHAPTER 1

actionable insights, practical tips, and real-life examples to help you navigate the challenges of a layoff and rediscover your professional potential. Whether you are looking to re-enter the job market, explore new career paths, or build a personal brand, this book will provide you with the tools and confidence to chart a path to success.

2

Chapter 1: The Shock of Layoff

The first day of a layoff hits like a ton of bricks. You wake up, feeling the absence of your daily routine, and a void that gnaws at your confidence. But it's normal to feel shaken. Acknowledge your emotions—be it shock, anger, or fear. It's crucial to face these feelings head-on, rather than suppressing them. Talking to friends, family, or a counselor can help you process these emotions and begin your journey of recovery.

Layoffs often leave individuals questioning their self-worth and professional abilities. It's a blow to the ego, making you doubt your skills and future. Instead of spiraling into negative self-talk, it's important to remind yourself that a layoff is not a personal failure but often a business decision beyond your control. Reframing your thoughts can help preserve your self-esteem and prepare you for the next steps.

In the initial days, create a small to-do list to regain a sense of control. Simple tasks such as updating your resume, organizing your workspace, or setting up informational interviews can keep you grounded. Taking these steps not only fills your day with productive activities but also symbolizes the beginning of your new chapter. Small accomplishments can provide a much-needed boost during this tumultuous period.

It's also a good time to reassess your financial situation. Create a budget and identify essential expenses, cutting out non-essentials. Understanding your financial runway can alleviate some of the immediate stress and help you plan your job search timeline. Seek professional financial advice if needed to ensure you're making informed decisions during this transition.

Lastly, give yourself permission to rest. The period immediately following a layoff can be emotionally and physically draining. Allow yourself to take a break, indulge in hobbies, and spend time with loved ones. This downtime is crucial for mental rejuvenation and can help you approach the job search with a fresh, positive mindset.

3

Chapter 2: Redefining Your Career Goals

A layoff can be a catalyst for re-evaluating your career goals. With the sudden change, you have an opportunity to reflect on what you truly want from your professional life. Begin by identifying your core values and what drives you. Are you passionate about a particular industry, or do you thrive in certain work environments? Understanding your motivations can help you set more meaningful career objectives.

Consider conducting a SWOT analysis of your career—identifying your Strengths, Weaknesses, Opportunities, and Threats. This exercise can provide clarity on where you excel and areas that need improvement. Additionally, it can help you recognize external opportunities that align with your strengths and how to navigate potential threats in your job search. Use this analysis to create a strategic plan for your next career move.

Networking becomes crucial during this phase. Reach out to former colleagues, mentors, and industry connections. Inform them of your current situation and express your interest in exploring new opportunities. Networking can uncover hidden job markets and lead to valuable insights and referrals. Attend industry events, join professional organizations, and engage in online forums to expand your network further.

Another aspect of redefining your career goals is upskilling. Identify any skills gaps that may hinder your progress and seek out training programs, certifications, or courses that can bridge these gaps. Continuous learning not only enhances your qualifications but also demonstrates your commitment to professional growth. This proactive approach can make you more competitive in the job market.

Lastly, consider alternative career paths. Sometimes, a layoff can open doors to new and unexpected opportunities. Explore industries or roles you may not have considered before. Your existing skills might be transferable to different fields, offering a fresh and exciting career trajectory. Stay open-minded and embrace the possibilities that come with change.

4

Chapter 3: Crafting Your Personal Brand

In today's competitive job market, personal branding is more important than ever. Your personal brand is how you present yourself to potential employers, colleagues, and industry peers. Start by creating a clear and compelling narrative of your professional journey. Highlight your achievements, skills, and unique value proposition. This narrative should be consistently reflected in your resume, LinkedIn profile, and other professional materials.

Developing an online presence is a key component of personal branding. Ensure your LinkedIn profile is polished and up-to-date. Share industry-related articles, participate in discussions, and showcase your expertise through thoughtful posts. Consider creating a personal website or blog where you can share insights, portfolio work, and testimonials. A strong online presence can help you stand out and attract potential employers.

Networking and relationship-building are also integral to personal branding. Attend networking events, webinars, and industry conferences to connect with professionals in your field. Be authentic and genuine in your interactions, and follow up with new connections to build lasting relationships. Personal referrals and recommendations can significantly enhance your job search and professional reputation.

Another aspect of personal branding is your professional image. Pay attention to your attire, communication style, and overall demeanor. First impressions matter, and presenting yourself confidently and professionally can leave a lasting impact. Seek feedback from trusted friends or mentors to ensure your image aligns with your personal brand.

Finally, leverage social proof to strengthen your brand. Request endorsements and recommendations from former colleagues, supervisors, and clients. Positive testimonials can validate your skills and experiences, adding credibility to your profile. Additionally, consider volunteering or taking on freelance projects to gain more testimonials and broaden your experience.

5

Chapter 4: Navigating the Job Market

The job market can be daunting, especially after a layoff. However, with a strategic approach, you can navigate it successfully. Start by identifying job opportunities that align with your redefined career goals. Use job search engines, company websites, and recruitment agencies to explore openings. Tailor your resume and cover letter for each application, highlighting relevant skills and experiences.

Consider leveraging online job search platforms like LinkedIn, Indeed, and Glassdoor. These platforms offer job listings, company reviews, and networking opportunities. Set up job alerts to stay informed about new openings in your field. Additionally, utilize the platform's features to connect with recruiters and hiring managers, increasing your visibility to potential employers.

Networking continues to play a crucial role in job hunting. Inform your professional network about your job search and seek referrals. Attend industry events and virtual job fairs to meet potential employers. Join professional associations and participate in online forums to expand your connections. Personal referrals often carry more weight than cold applications, increasing your chances of landing an interview.

Prepare thoroughly for job interviews. Research the company, understand its values, and align your responses with its mission. Practice common interview questions and develop STAR (Situation, Task, Action, Result) responses to highlight your accomplishments. Be confident and articulate your value proposition clearly. Remember, interviews are not just about the employer assessing you but also an opportunity for you to evaluate if the company is the right fit for you.

Stay resilient and patient throughout the job search process. Rejections are part of the journey, and it's essential to learn from each experience. Seek feedback when possible, and continuously improve your approach. Celebrate small victories, such as securing an interview or receiving positive feedback. Maintain a positive mindset and trust that the right opportunity will come along.

6

Chapter 5: Leveraging Gig Economy and Freelancing

In recent years, the gig economy and freelancing have gained significant traction. Post-layoff, these options can provide financial stability and diverse work experiences. Explore freelance platforms like Upwork, Fiverr, and Freelancer to find short-term projects that match your skills. These platforms offer opportunities across various industries, allowing you to work on projects that align with your expertise.

Freelancing offers flexibility, enabling you to manage your time and workload. It allows you to build a portfolio of work, showcasing your capabilities to potential employers. Additionally, freelancing can lead to long-term contracts or even full-time job offers. Approach each project with professionalism and deliver high-quality results to build a positive reputation in the freelance community.

The gig economy also includes part-time and temporary work opportunities. Consider roles such as consulting, tutoring, or temp jobs to supplement your income. These positions can provide valuable experience and help you stay engaged in the workforce. Temporary roles can sometimes lead to permanent positions, offering a pathway back to full-time employment.

Networking is equally important in the gig economy. Connect with other freelancers, join online communities, and attend industry events. Building a

CHAPTER 5: LEVERAGING GIG ECONOMY AND FREELANCING

network of fellow freelancers can lead to collaborations, referrals, and new project opportunities. Additionally, seek feedback from clients to improve your skills and enhance your service offerings.

Finally, continuously market yourself as a freelancer. Create a professional website, update your portfolio, and actively promote your services on social media. Share testimonials and success stories to attract new clients. By establishing a strong online presence and leveraging your network, you can thrive in the gig economy and turn freelancing into a sustainable career option.

7

Chapter 6: Exploring Alternative Career Paths

A layoff can be an opportunity to explore alternative career paths. Sometimes, a different industry or role may align better with your skills and interests. Begin by researching industries that are growing and have a demand for your skillset. Healthcare, technology, renewable energy, and e-commerce are examples of sectors that offer diverse career opportunities.

Consider taking career assessments or consulting with a career coach to identify potential paths. These tools can provide insights into your strengths and interests, guiding you toward suitable alternatives. Explore job shadowing or informational interviews to gain a better understanding of different roles. These experiences can help you make informed decisions about your next career move.

Transferable skills play a crucial role in transitioning to a new career. Identify skills from your previous roles that can be applied to different industries. Communication, project management, and analytical skills are examples of transferable skills that are valued across various sectors. Highlight these skills in your resume and cover letter to demonstrate your versatility to potential employers.

Upskilling or reskilling may be necessary when transitioning to a new

CHAPTER 6: EXPLORING ALTERNATIVE CAREER PATHS

career. Enroll in training programs, courses, or certifications that are relevant to your desired field. Many online platforms offer affordable and accessible learning options. Investing in education can continue providing additional skills and knowledge, which can significantly enhance your employability. Additionally, volunteering or part-time work in your new field can provide practical experience and help you build a network within the industry.

Networking remains a valuable tool when exploring alternative career paths. Attend industry events, webinars, and seminars to connect with professionals in your desired field. Inform your network about your career transition and seek advice and referrals. Networking can lead to valuable insights and potential job opportunities that may not be advertised.

Lastly, stay patient and open-minded during this transition. Changing careers can be challenging and may take time. Celebrate small milestones and remain persistent in your efforts. Embrace the learning process and view each experience as a stepping stone toward your new career.

8

Chapter 7: Building a Support System

A strong support system is essential during your career recovery journey. Surround yourself with positive and supportive individuals who can provide encouragement and guidance. Friends, family, mentors, and career coaches can offer valuable perspectives and help you stay motivated. Share your goals and progress with them, and don't hesitate to seek their advice when needed.

Joining support groups or online communities for individuals who have experienced layoffs can be beneficial. These groups provide a platform to share experiences, exchange job search tips, and offer emotional support. Being part of a community can help reduce feelings of isolation and provide a sense of camaraderie.

Consider working with a career coach or counselor to navigate your job search and career transition. Career coaches can provide personalized guidance, help you set achievable goals, and offer strategies for overcoming challenges. They can also assist with resume writing, interview preparation, and networking techniques. Investing in professional support can significantly enhance your job search success.

Additionally, engage in self-care practices to maintain your mental and physical well-being. Regular exercise, a balanced diet, and sufficient sleep are crucial for overall health. Mindfulness and relaxation techniques, such as meditation or yoga, can help reduce stress and improve focus. Taking care of yourself ensures you remain resilient and energized throughout your career recovery journey.

Finally, celebrate your achievements, no matter how small. Acknowledge the progress you make and reward yourself for your efforts. Positive reinforcement can boost your confidence and motivation, helping you stay on track toward your career goals.

Chapter 8: Preparing for Interviews

Effective interview preparation is key to securing your next job. Start by researching the company and understanding its values, culture, and mission. Familiarize yourself with the job description and identify the key skills and experiences required for the role. Tailor your responses to align with the company's needs and demonstrate how you can add value.

Practice common interview questions and develop STAR (Situation, Task, Action, Result) responses to highlight your achievements. This structured approach ensures you provide clear and concise answers while showcasing your skills and experiences. Additionally, prepare questions to ask the interviewer about the role, team, and company culture. Thoughtful questions demonstrate your interest and engagement.

Pay attention to your non-verbal communication during the interview. Maintain eye contact, smile, and use confident body language. Dress appropriately for the interview, considering the company's dress code and culture. A professional appearance can leave a positive impression on the interviewer.

Conduct mock interviews with a friend, mentor, or career coach to receive constructive feedback. Practicing in a simulated environment can help you refine your responses and reduce interview anxiety. Take note of areas for improvement and work on them before the actual interview.

CHAPTER 8: PREPARING FOR INTERVIEWS

Finally, follow up with a thank-you email after the interview. Express your gratitude for the opportunity and reiterate your interest in the role. A thoughtful follow-up can leave a lasting impression and set you apart from other candidates.

10

Chapter 9: Negotiating Job Offers

Receiving a job offer is a significant milestone, but it's essential to approach negotiations with confidence and preparation. Start by researching industry standards and salary benchmarks for the role you're being offered. Websites like Glassdoor, Payscale, and LinkedIn can provide valuable insights into typical salary ranges and compensation packages.

Before entering negotiations, identify your priorities and must-haves. Consider factors such as salary, benefits, work-life balance, professional development opportunities, and company culture. Having a clear understanding of your priorities will help you make informed decisions during negotiations.

When discussing salary, be prepared to articulate your value proposition and the unique skills you bring to the role. Highlight your achievements and experiences that align with the company's needs. Be confident in your worth, but also be open to compromise and finding a mutually beneficial agreement.

In addition to salary, consider negotiating other aspects of the job offer. This may include signing bonuses, relocation assistance, flexible work arrangements, and professional development opportunities. Ensure that the overall package aligns with your career goals and personal needs.

Once you've reached an agreement, review the offer letter carefully before accepting. Ensure that all negotiated terms are clearly stated in writing. If any discrepancies arise, address them promptly with the employer. Accepting the offer with confidence and clarity sets a positive tone for your new role.

11

Chapter 10: Onboarding and Settling In

Starting a new job can be both exciting and nerve-wracking. To ease the transition, take proactive steps to settle into your new role. Begin by familiarizing yourself with the company's onboarding process and resources. Attend orientation sessions, complete necessary paperwork, and engage with training materials.

Introduce yourself to your new colleagues and build relationships within your team. Be approachable, show enthusiasm, and actively participate in team activities. Building positive connections early on can create a supportive work environment and help you feel more comfortable in your new role.

Take the initiative to learn about the company's culture, values, and goals. Understanding the organizational dynamics can help you navigate your new workplace effectively. Seek feedback from your supervisor and colleagues to ensure you're meeting expectations and contributing positively to the team.

Set clear goals and priorities for your first few months on the job. Create a plan to achieve these goals and track your progress. Regularly communicate with your supervisor to discuss your achievements and seek guidance. Demonstrating your commitment and proactive approach can establish a strong foundation for your career growth within the company.

Finally, be patient with yourself as you adjust to your new role. It's normal to encounter challenges and uncertainties during the transition period. Stay positive, seek support when needed, and trust that you will adapt and thrive

CHAPTER 10: ONBOARDING AND SETTLING IN

in your new position.

12

Chapter 11: Continuous Learning and Growth

Career recovery doesn't end with landing a new job. Continuous learning and growth are essential for long-term success. Stay updated with industry trends and advancements by attending conferences, webinars, and workshops. Engaging in lifelong learning ensures you remain competitive and adaptable in a rapidly changing job market.

Seek out professional development opportunities within your organization. Volunteer for challenging projects, take on leadership roles, and pursue additional training or certifications. Proactively seeking growth opportunities demonstrates your commitment to your career and can lead to promotions and increased responsibilities.

Networking remains valuable even after you've secured a job. Continue to build and maintain relationships with industry professionals, colleagues, and mentors. Networking can provide valuable insights, support, and potential career opportunities in the future. Stay active in professional associations and online communities to stay connected and informed.

Reflect on your career goals periodically and assess your progress. Set new objectives and create a plan to achieve them. Whether it's advancing within your current organization or exploring new opportunities, having a clear vision for your career path keeps you motivated and focused.

CHAPTER 11: CONTINUOUS LEARNING AND GROWTH

Finally, prioritize work-life balance to ensure long-term well-being. Establish boundaries between work and personal life, and make time for activities that bring you joy and relaxation. Maintaining a healthy work-life balance enhances your overall quality of life and contributes to sustained career success.

13

Chapter 12: Embracing the Future

Your journey from layoff to career recovery is a testament to your resilience and determination. Embrace the future with confidence, knowing that you've navigated challenging times and emerged stronger. Reflect on the lessons learned and the growth you've experienced throughout this journey.

Stay adaptable and open to new opportunities. The job market and workplace dynamics are constantly evolving, and being flexible allows you to thrive in changing environments. Embrace change as an opportunity for growth and continue to seek out new challenges and experiences.

Give back to others who may be experiencing similar challenges. Share your story, offer support, and provide guidance to those navigating their career recovery journey. Your experiences can inspire and empower others to overcome their own obstacles and achieve their goals.

Celebrate your achievements and milestones along the way. Recognize the hard work, perseverance, and dedication that have brought you to this point. Each accomplishment, no matter how small, is a step toward your continued success.

As you move forward, remember that career recovery is an ongoing process. Stay proactive, maintain a positive mindset, and continue to invest in your personal and professional growth. Embrace the future with optimism, knowing that you have the strength and resilience to overcome any challenges

CHAPTER 12: EMBRACING THE FUTURE

that come your way.

Book Description: From Layoff to Lift Up: Career Recovery Map

Navigating the aftermath of a layoff can be one of the most challenging experiences in a professional's life. "From Layoff to Lift Up: Career Recovery Map" is a comprehensive guide designed to help you not only recover but thrive in your career after experiencing a layoff. This book is a beacon of hope, offering practical advice, actionable strategies, and inspiring insights to turn your setback into a powerful comeback.

Inside this book, you will discover:

- **Emotional Resilience**: Learn how to process and manage the emotional impact of a layoff. Understand that it is a natural part of the journey and find ways to stay positive and motivated.
- **Redefining Career Goals**: Use this unexpected change as an opportunity to reassess your career aspirations. Identify your strengths, explore new industries, and set meaningful objectives that align with your values.
- **Personal Branding**: Craft a compelling personal brand that stands out in a competitive job market. From creating a standout resume to building a strong online presence, this book provides the tools you need to present yourself confidently to potential employers.
- **Job Market Navigation**: Gain insights into effective job search strategies, networking techniques, and leveraging online job platforms. Learn how to uncover hidden job markets and accelerate your job search.
- **Gig Economy and Freelancing**: Explore the benefits of freelancing and gig opportunities. Discover how to find short-term projects that match your skills, build a successful freelance career, and achieve financial stability.
- **Career Transitioning**: Identify transferable skills and explore alternative career paths. Develop a strategic plan for transitioning to a new industry or role, and embrace the possibilities of a fresh career trajectory.
- **Support System Building**: Understand the importance of a strong support system. Seek guidance from friends, family, mentors, and career coaches to stay motivated and focused on your recovery journey.

- **Interview Preparation and Job Offer Negotiation**: Master the art of interviewing and negotiating job offers. Prepare thoroughly, articulate your value proposition, and confidently navigate the negotiation process.
- **Continuous Learning and Growth**: Embrace lifelong learning and professional development. Stay updated with industry trends, seek growth opportunities, and maintain a healthy work-life balance to ensure long-term success.
- **Future Planning**: Reflect on the lessons learned, celebrate your achievements, and stay adaptable to new opportunities. Embrace the future with optimism and confidence, knowing that you have the resilience to overcome any challenges.

"From Layoff to Lift Up: Career Recovery Map" is not just a guidebook; it's a companion on your journey to career recovery. Filled with actionable insights, real-life examples, and practical tips, this book will empower you to rebuild your career, achieve your goals, and emerge stronger than ever before. Whether you are looking to re-enter the job market, explore new career paths, or build a personal brand, this book provides the roadmap to success.

www.ingramcontent.com/pod-product-compliance
Lightning Source LLC
LaVergne TN
LVHW010444070526
838199LV00066B/6179